PRAISE FOR *Held and Firmly Bound*

The starting point of Claudia Rankine's theory of the Racial Imaginary is the conviction that "our imaginations are creatures as limited as we ourselves are," and that "every act of imaginative sympathy inevitably has limits." In *Held and Firmly Bound,* Nathalie Anderson, a white poet of Southern origins, concurs, even as she charges into territory that is rife with racial stereotypes prevalent in the canonical literature of the American South. Pinning her poem to an actual ancestral document from 1853 which records a large debt owed to Betsey Garrett, "a free person of color," Anderson tries to poetically conjure the real life Betsey without presuming the typical appropriations of persona poetry. Thus, instead of the imagined, ventriloquial voice of Betsey Garrett, Anderson gives us a series of oblique glimpses of her from the perspective of the white people among whom she lived as they sought to understand the origins of her freedom and the source of her power in the antebellum era – a freed slave, a wronged woman, a holder of white secrets, a source of white guilt, an extraordinary, marketable talent. Part narrative poem, part lyric interrogation, part historical investigation, concerned with both the sociology and metaphysics of race, and at all times, profoundly psychological, *Held and Firmly Bound* keeps bringing us back to Anderson's central point: that each of is "held and firmly bound" by the consciousness inscribed within our own imaginations, and by the inevitable revelation of that consciousness through our utterance. A fascinating collection.

--Kate Daniels, author of *A Walk in Victoria's Secret*

Located at the intersection of family and region, Nathalie Anderson's sequence of magnificently wrought lyric poems seeks to determine how a distant relative, one M.D. Huger, came to be indebted to a free woman of color named Betsey Garrett for the princely sum of $2400. The language in these wonderfully luminous poems helps the reader to imagine the variety of circumstances that may have led up to the transaction. Endeavoring to illuminate the "complicated possibilities," of such an extraordinary state of affairs, Anderson's chapbook achieves on multiple levels: gesturing toward the many forms human frailty can assume while insisting that it is only through sustained acts of truthmaking that matters such as these can yield up their redemptive potential. A singular achievement whose implications are impossible to deny.

--Herman Beavers, author of *Obsidian Blues*

Held and Firmly Bound

Held and Firmly Bound

by

Nathalie Anderson

Muddy Ford Press
Chapin, South Carolina

Held and Firmly Bound. Copyright 2017 by Nathalie Anderson. All rights reserved. Printed in the United States of America. No part of this book may be used or reproduced in any manner whatsoever without written permission except in the case of brief quotations embodied in critical articles and reviews. For information please contact Muddy Ford Press, 1009 Muddy Ford Road, Chapin, SC.

MuddyFordPress.com

Library of Congress Number:2017901573

ISBN: 978-1-942081-10-4

KNOW ALL MEN BY THESE PRESENTS, THAT I,
Alfred H. Dunkin, Trustee of M. D. Huger,
am held and firmly bound unto Betsey Garrett,
a free person of color, in the full and just sum of
Two Thousand Four Hundred Dollars....

                                              Charleston, 1853

This family document, this record of indebtedness, has arrested and gripped me since it came to me after my father's death in 1998. How did a white Carolinian come to owe such an extraordinary debt to a free person of color – a *woman* of color – seven years before the Civil War? Like most IOUs, this very formal document doesn't say. Its conventional legal language, by which the debtor is "held and firmly bound" to transfer funds, resonates disturbingly in an era when persons of color were often all too literally "held" and "bound." Yet the document also hints at complex relations between these persons of different races. What – beyond the obvious, the pledge and ultimate payment of a financial obligation – might these legal formulations signify?

And the debt *is* extraordinary. I've often been asked how much this $2400 would be worth today, but historians tell me that's not the best question: rather, we might ask what that money might do, what it might buy. In wills from that era, a man might bequeath to his wife his Charleston house with $500 intended to provide for its upkeep, presumably in perpetuity. Or someone might leave a bequest to a slave or former slave, most likely something like $25 or $50.

The price of a slave at the time ranged from around $500 to perhaps $1450.

We might imagine Betsey Garrett as a freed slave, remembered with a sizable stipend after the slave owner's death, perhaps with the intention of enabling her to buy out of slavery a husband or a child. Or we might imagine Betsey Garrett as an entrepreneur, a free and independent person who perhaps sold goods or loaned money to white Carolinians, and required repayment of the "full and just sum" owed her. Or we might imagine a more intimate bond: how enticing (and how disquieting) it is to read the legal phrase "held and firmly bound" in this light, opening complicated possibilities – that she's being paid for damages after an assault, or for child support after a liaison, or for her silence after someone's indiscretion. At a time when most Southern blacks were legally powerless, what "hold" might Betsey Garrett have had that would have "bound" a white person to pay her so significant a sum?

Whatever we might imagine, I believe that the white populace of Betsey Garrett's time would have been imagining her, too – projecting their limited understanding, their fears and their desires, onto the persons of color surrounding them. Accordingly, I haven't put words into Betsey Garrett's mouth in this sequence, but rather have tried to imagine how those in her debt might have imagined her. Here, the person who owes appears as man or as woman, as bystander or as lover or as attacker, as fervent or as equivocal emancipator, each finding in the figure of Betsey Garrett a reflection of his or her own longing, terror, perplexity, magnanimity, and shame. And the thought-provoking phrase "held and firmly bound" echoes through other contexts, inviting us to consider how it signifies for us as well.

Held and Firmly Bound

Contents

Say / 5

Held / 19

Plus / 37

SAY:

1.

Let's say you're your mama's littlest lamb
and when she goes, they lose you. Night after night
in your ceaseless seeking, you leg yourself limp,
bleat yourself brittle. There's no availing.

Or say you're your mama's fair-haired child.
Through all your picking in the pantry, your
flouncings round the yard, your wrigglings and
your snivelings at prayers, she doesn't
hear a word against you, no, it's "Oh!
the cherub cheeks" or "Oh! the haloing of curls,"
and so the kicking up, the biting down, and
when she goes they let you flail all night,
they let your squalling face go blue.

Or say you're a mama's boy, and when she goes
they ship you off soft, thinking to harden you.
Smaller and smaller as the road twists
you away, you shrink so they can handle you, man-
handle you, those gentle men. You know to speak
when spoken to, so every nudge and nick, each
gouge and goad, each punch and thrust, you answer
"sir," you butter-won't-melt, you devil-may-care:
the harder they hit, the more you can't cry.

Yes, you're the golden boy. Everything you touch,
you're good for it. You live large, live larger, are
largesse. You can bank on it. You can bet
your life. You can bet your expectations. You
can bet the farm. Hit me, you say to the man
with the cards. Hit me hard. Hit me again.

Or say you're your mama's little man, and
when she goes she grips your arms, she looks you
up and down. She needs you tall, she needs you
grown. You'll stand for her. You're all she owns.
But when you fall? But when you fall?

No, still and all, you're the mammy's boy, she who never leaves, she who's there for you, she who mustn't snap, she who shakes her head, she who can't say no. Who pinches cheeks, who bites her coins, who bides her time, who grows a thing that grows a thing. And if not she, if far from she, some other she, some Bess or Bits, some Betsey, who makes things cook, who bides your time, who knows a man who knows a man. Where else would you turn? How much do you owe?

2.

Let's say you're a sweet girl, the tidying kind,
and after a while that tidiness grows, say,
fastidious. You wash morning and night, and
not just the face and hands, not just the bright parts
that show. You flannel yourself, scrub at your nails,
scour the ears, rinse with nettles the hair. There's
water set to boiling morning and night, poured
clear into your white china bowl. You'll wear down
the house help, your mother swears, what with all that
fetch and carry, all that hauling of your suds.

Miss Prissy. Miss Primness. You hear what they say.
Your mother calls you finicking. Your daddy
brings you soft soaps, brings you violet water,
brings ribbons left sunning til they're light as cream.
He calls you his sweet girl. Sweet's just what you are.
But the flesh was ever a tribulation –
the body staled with sleep or soured with strain;
the foot gone rank, closed for hours in its shoe;
the hair gone rancid, shaken loose from its nets;
the underarms gone musty. Not to mention

what we never mention – the reek of your slops,
the thick stench of your blood, the sudden hot stink
that rises from nowhere whenever you're galled.
Some days you're so shamed you won't stir from your room
no matter how hard your mother slaps her palm
against the jamb. You wash out your smalls. You dip
your feet to the ankles every chance you get.
You wring out your skirts where they draggle the floor.
Your mother fumes and frets, scolds and chides, but your
daddy chivies her, says "Mother, let her be."

And then – let's say – the sickness takes him, and you
set all that aside. Like a miasma, stench
seeps from the sickroom, stench rises like steam
up the stairs, yet you carry and fetch, even
his slops, even his sweated shirts. Your own clothes
reek with it no matter how long you air them,
yet, while your mother steadies his head, you hold

the bowl that holds his bile. You breathe through your mouth
to stay by his side. You carry sachets. You
wipe with cool cloths his feverish face. "Sweet girl,"

he says, and you think it's the end. "Sweet girl, there's
a sweet thing I need you to do." And you do,
you sweet girl, though your mother can't know: you go –
once he's gone – through streets rank with dung, rank with rot,
past the brackish docks to the lawyer's rooms. And
how strange to meet there the girl scrubbed so shiny
and braided so tight she could be your own twin,
strange to scent within that rich womanly musk
the faintest familiar taint of her raw wound,
the faintest familiar wash of violet air.

3.

Let's say you're a mean man, a mean rapscallion.
You've grown up mean. Or you're born that way. It happens.

Could be the pater's a stickler and the mater a scythe,
and between them they've sliced you about. Could be
the father's a shirk and the mother a shrike, and you've
blown back and forth between them. Could be the pa's
a rakehell and the ma's a hellion, and you've gone to ground
just like they showed you. Or the mama's rich
and the daddy's good-looking, and with all that tending,
all that looking past or through you, you learned early
to dissemble. The baby pinched blue. The dung flung down
where the passing skirt will catch it. The muddy thrust
to the mouth to the eye. The chokehold on the critter.
All down to you. Know how the gator rests in the muck
showing no more than its eye? Know how the rattler
suns in the duff? how the shark crests with the wave?
No way to see what all you've done.

                                        And a good thing, too,
seeing how this turned out. The red creeping up your neck
your face flushed with the drink the angry. Who'd think
they'd care, given where and who you struck? She has
that money now. She won't have it long. No, when all this
fining's done, you've got yourself a list, starting with
judges and lawyers, and that Betsey Garrett, and your pops
always swinging his rod, and your moms always washing
you off her hands.

4.

Say you're what folks call up-country, down
from the red-clay hills, in Charleston
for the Season, settled at your Aunt Em's,
and about the serious business – or so
your mama tells – of finding you
a proper man. Now, about that
you've got some ideas of your own, but
your mama's having none of them. Before
you leave, she takes your face in her hands
to best impart her most emphatic word, and you
have promised, sincerely promised her,
you will do as best you can.

Thus far, truth be told, your best ain't
up to snuff. First off, you've grown out
raw-boned, rangy, stark as a mule
in a paddock of ponies, nothing like
your flirty cousins. Next to them, your hair's
a shock, your knuckles scuffed, your cheek
freckled up from too much sun, and what
your mama stitched for you, painstaking,
all the summer long, shows next to theirs
like what a mama wears, or might have wore
in her young days in town. Them cousins
is all polite up front, but they titter
behind their fans. Even the gal who
sets your clothes out knows what's what.
She smirks when she thinks you're not looking.
She sucks in her cheeks like something
amusing's stuck back there. Well, about all that,
you got some ideas for making a change.

"Gal," you say, and you watch her clench up,
knowing she's been caught out, not knowing
what you might do, and you let her squirm –
as your mama says, for true, this
teasing of those less fortunate
is not your kindest way. "Gal," you say,
"you got a discerning eye, so you
can see I ain't. But I got hold of a thing
you might appreciate. What say we trade?"

What you done with her then is not
the law, some even say it's sin, but
she takes it up fast, being flash
as a pin and twice as scratchy,
and you so practiced at it,
lettering for the neighbors' daughters,
setting them straight with only the good book
and a bit of chalk and slate. And in return
she done you up right, hacking out
the bramble of your hair, smoothing it
down in front and twirling it back
behind. She sprinkles your cheeks with
the faintest talc, then feathers it
nearly all away. And cloth is cloth,
so once she's ripped them frocks apart
and pieced them back, they prance just fine,
and you show about as pretty
as ever you could do. No man, of course –
not many these days take to your
mulish kind – but seeing for herself
how smart you are, you think your mama
will be satisfied.

As for that gal, after all these works,
you know her name and you call her by it.
"Betsey Garrett," you say, while she's
packing up your clothes, "I am my mama's
only living child, and when I come
into my own, I'm going to buy you out,
set you on your road." She rolls them eyes.
She knows by now your teasing ways.
"Betsey Garrett," you say, "furthermore,
I hate them cousins and I owe you, gal,
and when at last I go to my reward
I'll leave you everything I've come to own."
She rolls them eyes. You're such a quiz.
She mocks you back: "What'll I do then?"
She's smiling, playing that massa game. You
hold up a day-dress, its fine-stitched top,
its splurge of skirts, the way the rose flows
over the cream. "About that," you say,
"I see you got some ideas of your own."

5.

Say it's your land, was always your land, or
anyhow your father's land, or land he
always swore would somehow anyhow come
some day to you. A man's got rights. What's his
stays his, in the eternal eyes of God –
so you believe, and so your father swears.

A man's got rights. In Ireland, you've heard tell,
was penal laws: back then, no one owned land
if the law held them less than men – no Pope-ish lands,
and that's as should be. Laws should serve whole men,
your father says, and let idolaters
go hang. A man's got rights. There should be laws.

Yet there she squats in her rackety shack,
a heathen, surely. An idolater.
She's filched the title off him. Your father
can't say how. There should be laws. It's your land
and your father swears you'll seize it, steal it,
buy it back, if it's the last thing he makes you do.

6.

Say it's your land. You made it so. Dredged out
the silted stream. Plowed the swamp muck under.
Husbandry. (Your eyes, she said, like a jay,
she said, blithe in a shaft of sunlight).

By June, despite the hat, your face
is brick-clay red; by August, seamed oak-brown.
Despite the boots, your toe-nails blacken.
Free hold. There's nothing free about it.

Strange how what's strengthened you will sap another,
how Lily wilted and Rose shriveled –
which is to say, one fevered down, one shrank
into the third hard birthing. With Violet,

you changed your will to read "my wife": "I leave
to my wife my house in town." Why name her
when she's fading, too? (Blue eyes, she said,
like a jay, she said, and just as raucous).

Cholera. Malaria. The one son drowns.
Your brother frails. You auction off his goods.
Say it's your land. Say it all you want.
Raise your meaty arms. Brace your tree-trunk legs.

At your brother's place, a house boy and
a field hand look away from you
with your brother's eyes. They're raking out
the kitchen garden, setting tenderly

the seed. Husbandry. You won't claim them,
but you see their claim. (Sun in the pines.
The flying jay). Your brother kept them close;
freed the mother, kept her close that way. You

won't deed it, won't gift it, won't acknowledge
who they might be, but suppose you pose it
as a debt paid – the world won't question that.
You can close that book. You can walk away.

With so much cash, she can buy what she wants,
buy the boys free, work the land themselves.
Say it's her land now. She can say it's so.
(Jay on the wing. A sunlit jay).

7.

Let's suppose there's somewhat needs doing. Let's suppose
there's somewhat needs done. Say it's not what can be spoke
to wife nor preacher, not what can be posted up,
or shouted in the street, or telegraphed, but what's
done nudge by nudge, and who you nudge, and who then
nudges who. Not a ditch what needs digging, though there's
ditching to come. Not a hog what needs dressing, though
somewhat's bound to spill. You won't dirty your hands. You
need some who what will. Say you nudge up some nudged
       who.
How then do you pay?

Sure there's coin in the pocket. Slapped on the barrel.
Slipped under the table. Spun into air. But who
couldn't see there's hell to come, and payback striding
down the road? The who you nudge is canny, wants
the law to back and brace him while he sidesteps the law

and you. Call it a debt, he says, a debt you'll owe
his mother or his sister or his wife, and what
or who she buys, and where they high-tail off to, you
don't have to know or see or say or do. Suppose
you call it proxy for proxy. Or a shut eye
for a shuttered eye. Or call it what it is: call it
a life for a life.

8.

Suppose you've sickened. No one knows why.

Suppose you shiver in full sun. When the night breeze rises
cool off the water, suppose the flesh sweats off you, suppose
you sear the soothing hand. The eyes burn, the lips shrivel.
     When
they hold out your mirror, suppose you see a staring skull.

And you shake like something's taken hold of rib and femur,
banging the bones about, breaking them down, bashing you
from the inside out. Your bruised lungs. Your beaten heart.

Say a word slippers into the sick room, you think maybe
a doctor's word, likely *conscious, unconscious*. Or was it
a preacher's word, his prayers mothing and fraying, yes
     that word
would be *conscience*. Or was it a lawyer's, speaking over
and past you, call it *contract* or *context*, stitching you in;
or was it a visiting lady's, breathy with *culture*?

No. Suppose it's nothing you've met yet, a mere breath
off the air, but you can't now not hear it: let's call it *conjure*.

Money's nothing. You can sell a horse, sell a house, sell off
a scrap of swampy ground. Suppose something out there
     claims you.
Blames you. Pay her off. Get her out of your head. Get her
     off your back.

9.

Say it's that moment when every limb
leafs out, when the grasses sprig up pert
and pearly, when the high pines swoon
with jessamine, gasping out great gusts
of pollinated sigh. Fast as that
the thin copse thickets, the open grove
closes over, wood shades to deep forest –
though in the black back there white petals drift,
a lace veil frayed to bits and pieces.

And then, as if Daphne reconsidered, turned
in her bark, reached out her leafy hand,
a sapling sashaying back into sunlight, bird-eyed:

      Dryad.

She's a secret you'll keep, and keep, and keep.
Anything and everything, you swore
when first you saw. The years accrue.
Now you're dying. Now, coward, now you can.

HELD:

1.

Her heart kept startling, a nervy bird, clutch
of blue at the breast, her fingers' twining and
intertwining fretting up the shakiest of nests.

His arm snaking round and his hand hovering –
she knew he'd swallow her down. Knew he'd keep her
own hands flustering til held and firmly bound.

2.

Out from the woods to sun on the rocks
they come, as autumn falls, and you can't tell
the chatter of leaves from their rattle of warning:
with what slow steps along the mined hillside
through springs coiled tight and ready to volley.

Yet by God's grace the preacher takes them up
so confidently, so casually, so quick,
a lightning bolt in each hand, held and firmly bound.

3.

You know this postcard. Blake. A shock-haired man
and a despondent woman, stripped stark, chained
back to back, he shout-mouthed, compressed
to a spring, she limp, a counterweight dangling slack.

And must she drag the chain? Six months since you split,
this card: "If you needed me, I would have come,"
meaning he'd needed, and you, cold-hearted bitch, had not
intuited or reached out or returned. Meaning don't forget:
in his world, where back is front, you're permanently,
til death might part you, held and firmly bound.

4.

Old gold, rose-gold, rolled rich and thick, a pastry
of a ring, what she'd always said she wanted,
and a dress of lace, lace over lace, the skirts
belled out and hooped and crinolined and trailing,
catching up the petals she walked over, so
by the time she reached the altar, the hem glowed rose

or reddened like she'd walked through blood to get there,
like she'd chopped off her toe or shaved down her heel
to fit the shoe. In her dreams that night, the ring
slipped over her, staving her like a barrel,
choking in her skirts, strangling her with briars:
by what she'd said she'd wanted, held and firmly bound.

5.

In the corner, a thickening, a bulking out,
a hulking up, a sharpening and unsheathing.
And on the stairs, a creak, and then another creak.
At the window, a quick tap, and then another.
How many of them are there? What do they want you for?

Lie breathless to discern them, a marbled effigy,
though death itself won't save you. Roll slow as a log
in a slow river, submerged between bed and wall,
though the slightest ripple betrays you. Slip somehow
under the bed, though – lurking, festering – who knows

what you'll meet down there. Or you might spring up swinging,
cudgel about with shirts and books and parasols,
all your limp detritus, your little fists beating
the evasive air. How do you master Proteus?
Get a grip, right? til each vagrant fear is held and firmly bound.

6.

Enchained in Paris, the Marquis imagines
chaining; caned, imagines caning; stained,
imagines that. Everything's reversible,

and not just in that shifty shift from doing
to being done, being done to doing. What
on your body I enact – he tells servants,

he tells mistresses, even as they leave him – I
feel reciprocally, as if inflicted: each slash,
each welt, each wound, each penetration

awakens my own flesh, and opens it –
a greedy feeding of the nerve. The Buddhist
does it too, he says (or might have said): swallows

what's offered, relishes the tiger's bite. Why
abandon with abandon the abandoned, when
distinctions waver and meander so

between abasing and abased, each party
to the torturing enmeshed in it, defined by it,
enhanced, diminished, held and firmly bound.

7.

A gothic tale: the roadhouse where the food's
poison, the bed's so hard it snaps the spine,
and the traveler who revels half the night
disappears entirely by morning.
Just such a host is Lavinia Fisher.
Huckster or broker, jobber or monger, she'll
chat you til you brag out your securities –
the deed in the lining, the coin in the heel,
the bag's false bottom – then send you off
to sleep, she says, with a cup of strychnine.
The one man who, not wanting to insult her,
spilled out his drink behind her back, lived to see
her knife his bed, and flung himself to safety then
from the second-story roadhouse window.

That's one tale. Here's another. Picture if you will
the Charleston Old Jail, all that brick and mortar
crumbling now, the great octagonal towers
fallen, the crenellations cracked, the iron bars
bowed out from all that weight: the narrowing cells,
the stark corridors, the stairs to nowhere.
They say she walks in there, cup in one hand,
knife in the other, hospitable as ever she was.
Did you think a woman on her way to hell like that
would just stay in her grave, held and firmly bound?

8.

Was Denmark Vesey framed? There's evidence
that a paltry politician, set to unseat
another paltry politician, invented
out of whole cloth Vesey's rebellion, thus
to indict his rival's slaves, thus to impugn
his rival's capacity to govern
them, or anyone. The other man, they say,
was gentler. With this proof – this so-called proof –
the politician won not only votes
but fears, and forged thus new Draconian laws
more congenial to his views: manumission
rescinded; free blacks requiring sponsors
to go anywhere, do anything; black sailors
peremptorily, prophylactically jailed.

How tempting to accept this explanation,
to fix the blame where we know blame belongs,
on the conniving, maligning, brutalizing
white. But if we do, what do we do
to Vesey? Do we not keep that bloody-
minded man – who, evidence suggests,
determined to revolt only when whites closed down
the African Methodist Episcopal church
he'd founded – do we not keep that passionate
and intelligent and righteous free man
held and firmly bound?

9.

The minié ball's a shatterer. Ask any sawbones.
The squat lead slugs don't look like much, but the powder's flare
swells them snug to the barrel, then rifles them through, spun
pissed and purposeful to whirlwind on impact: kneecaps
split, shins splintered, thigh-bones ground to powder, muscles
          ripped
raggedly away. Gut-shot or skull-shot, there's no hope
but blankets and morphine: the man dies or doesn't, it's
not in our hands, but otherwise.... Ask any sawbones
after a fourteen-hour day cutting in full sun –
longer if the moon's bright – wearying over his plank,
blood-stained, pus-soaked, knife sometimes in his teeth,
          grabbing out
for lancets, curettes, scalpels, bone saws, even chain saws,
the penis or the beard secured, tourniquet set, nerves
pulled taut and trimmed, the veins stitched shut with silk or
          horse-hair,
the bone scraped, then rasped smoother, the skin sometimes
          flapped down,
all in three minutes for a knee cut, ten for the thigh.
The limbs pile deep. Whitman at Fredericksburg saw enough
for "a full load for a one-horse cart." Men mostly didn't
bite the bullet, either, but slept thick, dreamed thicker, woke
to thirsts unquenchable, hazy. Stonewall Jackson heard
under ether ethereal music, thought later
it had to be the saw in the bone. But chloroform –
ask any sawbones – lets a man thrash before he calms,
so in his frenzy, like Jackson himself, the soldier
about to be halved must for his own damned good
be gripped by hefty helpers, held and firmly bound.

10.

Slaps him first, in outrage. This is not the boy
she raised. Sends him off to the changers
for the changing: change him back. Push him

to his knees, she tells them. Pray it out
or strike it out or scour him or break him
of it: whatever it takes, she wants

that rust gone, wants only the best
at her house, only the best for him.
And he comes back changed, so like new

he hurts the eyes, sanded and resurfaced
and detailed. Her friends envy her: so polite
her doubts bounce off him. Is she the only one

to hear his tinniness, his hesitations,
the thin times when his true colors maybe show?
Still waters. He'll never dance again for her

around the kitchen in his pjs, never
sing for her again, profundo then
falsetto. Happy now? He knows just what she wants and

gives just that to her. Meanwhile, deep below her prying,
he watches himself closer than Narcissus might,
still as God made him, good as he ever was,

a secret sweetly held and firmly bound.

11.

When an internationally celebrated actress
marries an independently wealthy man, the tabloids
yawn: old story. And if she's the scion and salvation
of British theatrical royalty, and he's loved her
the whole of her American tour, haunting stage doors, arms
full of flowers, pockets dripping with bracelets, handsome and
dashing and eager? Ho-hum. But what if she's a budding
abolitionist, and he, beyond his bankers, lives off
the backs of slaves? Philadelphia money: she thought bonds,
not bondage; and he loved her for her enthusiasms,
tuning out her prattlings, never thinking they might matter.
Her hackles, his eyebrows: all their stakes raised. One could
      print that.

We know what she saw in Georgia because she wrote it down:
the "sweltering lands and slimy waters"; the mosquitoes
so thick on a man's coat "that one could scarcely see the cloth,"
and men tied naked there for punishment; the "pittances"
of hominy, "tattered and filthy blankets"; babies left
"to crawl and kick in filthy cabins or on broiling sand";
the women by their labor "most broke in two"; the sick house
where – post-partum, emaciated, aged, chilled, fevered – they
lay "upon the hard cold ground"; an epileptic "barking
like some enraged animal"; the women forced; families
sold apart; girls, pregnant or just birthed, beaten in the fields
for malingering, or flogged, "clothes turned over their heads" –

"a procession of sable dreams." For fifteen weeks, she did
what little she could do: cleaned, sewed, served meat, paid
      black children
for their clean faces, requested rather than demanded,
paid slaves for any work done for her, taught the rudiments
of reading, appreciated, attended, respected,
advocated – though she knew teaching slaves was unlawful,
though she knew slaves were beaten for complaining to her,
      though
her husband – baffled, "morally muffled" – brushed her distress
away like a midge. She wished "the sea would swallow up
      and melt
in their salt waves" her husband's lands. She imagined "I
      should

consider my own throat and those of my children well cut"
should the slaves rise. "Their nakedness clothes me," she wrote,
      chastened.

Yet back in Philadelphia, even with all she knew,
she did not publish. Even after her husband was caught
in flagrante with another man's wife (and she learned this
through the tabloids), even after the divorce, even when
she'd returned to England, she kept her silence. Why? Because
the world was on his side. Because the lands weren't hers to sell,
the slaves weren't hers to free: she couldn't even promise them
"*That* thing shall not be done again." Because she believed
she should be able through love and reason to change his mind.
Because for nearly twenty-five years he kept their children
in his custody, well out of her reach, by the laws
of our good country conscientiously held and firmly bound.

12.

When Lafayette was imprisoned at Olmütz,
Francis Kinloch Huger, twenty-one-year-old
Carolinian, determined to free him.

I could tell this story so it's about youth –
Huger then, in fact, just two years older
than Lafayette when first he fought for us. Or

I could tell it so it's about legacy –
Huger's father's lands near Georgetown, in fact, where
Lafayette first came ashore, fearful the British
held Charleston – imagine, a nineteen-year-old
with a trans-Atlantic ship of his own! Or

I could tell it so it's about irony –
the slaves, fishing, who first encountered that ship
mistaking the French for brigands, and Lafayette
arguing with his hosts against slavery;
the sickly patriot boy – Huger – shipped where
but to England to be bettered; Lafayette –
who drafted the Rights of Man – branded traitor
by the Revolution, but in Austria
found treacherously revolutionary;
and – imprisoned – nevertheless, for his health,
sent out guarded twice a week on carriage rides.

Or I could tell it so it's about terror:
Lafayette's wife held in Paris, her *grandmère*
and *mère* and *soeur* all guillotined, their son Georges
Washington imperiled – this was no joke – but

I could tell it so it's all high-jinks – Huger
and his co-conspirator Bollman posing
as tourists at Olmütz, with nothing to see
but the prison, and writing back and forth to
Lafayette with no cipher but lemon juice; and

I could list out their slapstick blunders: how
one horse shied and galloped off; how one guard bit,
severely, Bollman; how when Huger shouted
"Ride for Hoff," Lafayette heard wrongly "Ride off,"
and rode off fast, entirely the wrong way; how
the strayed horse, recovered, balked at bearing two,
kicked up, threw both, stunned Bollman; how Lafayette
was recognized and caught; how Bollman, waiting
long at Hoff, was caught; how Huger, walking so
his friend could ride the skittish horse, was caught. Or

I could tell it tragically – the young men held
in irons for a year and tried for treason,
escaping narrowly Napoleon, who wished,
it seems, to kill them; Lafayette held five years
in all, so changed his own wife didn't know him
when she petitioned to share his cell, her health
broken too by the imprisonment. Or I

could tell it retrospectively, how Huger
and Lafayette met in 1824,
met as old friends yet really for the first time.
Lafayette – grateful, gracious – offered Huger
land. Huger refused. He had enough, he said,
and was teaching his sons to work for themselves.

All this is true as I can make it. But I
like better the story as I remember
my grandmother telling it: how two Huger
cousins – not true – took ship for France – not true – where
Lafayette, though imprisoned, rode out each day –
not true – on his very own horse – not true – and
when they came to free him, he said no – and though
this too is not true, for me it's still the heart
of the man and the matter – believing himself
by his own honor held and firmly bound.

13.

I saw *Glory* when it first came out, watched it
with critical distance like the cinephile I am, relishing
of course the performances – Denzel Washington twisted
 into resentment, André Braugher hurt
into discipline, Matthew Broderick shamed
into authority, Morgan Freeman watchful – but
doubting (as one does) the historicity.I mean, every movie
scants like this, skims two hours off months and years
and asks us to extrapolate the rest. No wonder they
take shortcuts: "Have you met Frederick Douglas?" No wonder
they offer us a tentfulof new soldiers to follow, or
anachronistically dismiss an idealistic man with "twit."

        Outside the movie, who today knows
Robert Gould Shaw, the young white man who led the 54th,
the first black regiment of the Civil War? Be honest: not us. We
must be introduced. And who's heard of William Carney, who
at Fort Wagner grabbed up the flag when the colors-bearer
was shot dead, and, though wounded twice himself, never
let it touch the ground? Yes, it's true: the earliest instance
of a black man earning the Medal of Honor, though given to him
forty years after the fact.

        That's Denzel Washington's role, though
in the film he refuses, the night before, to carry the whites' flag:
"I ain't fightin' this war for *you*, sir." Another shortcut: the cynic
who steps up, the protestor who ameliorates, rather than what
ever it was William Carney really felt or said – which to be fair
we can't now know. Hollywood's full of these shortcuts:
the wise advisor (Morgan Freeman), the soft aesthete who
grows into manly violence(André Braugher), the mouse
that roars (Matthew Broderick)....

        Yet with what fine skill the filmmakers
entice us to overlook these shortcuts, lose ourselves
in what feels logical, feels inexorable, feels real – for two hours,
anyhow. *Glory*'s better than most. Think what they've left out:
Carney's righteous pride in rescuing that flag; Shaw's bride
of eleven weeks who never marries again; Shaw's grieving father
who, learning his son lies buried "in the common trench with
the negroes,"writes to his friend, "What a body-guard he has!"

                  I won't go on. You can imagine how my mind
was turning as the film fought towards its end. Then, after
the carnage at Fort Wagner, we see a milky dawn sky, we see
the grey ocean, we see the pallid shore, and I realized
I'd been there; no, I mean *right* there, *just* there, there for real.
Leaving aside the unlikelihood (and in fact I was wrong; they
filmed *Glory*'s last scenes a state or two south of Charleston),
I knew

                  as well as I know my name
that shallow surf; the undertow that drags the sand; the sand
that steadies as the surf draws back, dimpling over buried cockles,
lavender, small as a little finger's nail; sand half dirt, half water,
that drips fluent from the hand to ornament sand turrets, castles,
forts; how the winds rise off the ocean, picking up that sand so
the body's sifted over, stung. Right there, I could feel it on me,
hear the waves churn, smell the salt sea.

                  Oh Quentin Compson, look away
all you please. There's one woman stopped cold as
the credits roll in Philly. That grit's in her teeth. That salt's
in her bones. No distance at all. By her own soil and substance,
held and firmly bound.

PLUS:

+ 1.

                      Betsey Garrett signs the papers not with an X
                      but with a +. Interest compounding.

Signifying: Cross hairs. Short hairs. Short straw.
                      Candles lit both ends. Irons in the fire.
                      Overstock. Over-run. Overboard. Eclipse.
                      Pay up, fool. You'll always owe me more.

                      An extra chair set fair to the table.
                      A coat that'll fit you, chit, once you grow out.
                      Beneath still waters, ice running dark.
                      Skin-deep? You don't know the half.

                      More than you bargained for, or you deserve.
                      Baker's dozen. Lagniappe. Sugar on top.
                      Shake on it. Shake with it. Can't shake it off.
                      Fist against hand. Hand into glove.

                      Saddled with. Hitched. Held. Bound.

HELD:

Section 3 references the Frontispiece to William Blake's *Visions of the Daughters of Albion*, first published in 1793.

Section 9 references Walt Whitman's *Specimen Days*, Chapter 22, "Down at the Front," an entry dated December 21, 1862. *Specimen Days* was first published in 1882.

Section 11 references Fanny Kemble's *Journal of a Residence on a Georgian Plantation in 1838-1839*, published in 1863.

Section 12 references *Statement of the Attempted Rescue of General Lafayette from "Olmutz,"* "prepared from the personal narrative and conversations of Col. F.K. Huger, by one of his family," "published and printed by Walker, Evans & Cogswell, 3 Broad Street, Charleston, S.C.," undated, but incorporating Huger's death in 1855.

Section 13 references the 1989 film *Glory*, directed by Edward Zwick.

$2400: I'm told by legal experts – and I too believe – that the amount owed would more likely be $1200, on the understanding that if $1200 were not paid by a certain date, the debtor would owe $2400. Whichever amount is accurate, it's an extraordinary debt for the time.

Acknowledgements:

HELD #7, under the title "Hauntings," *2014 Anthology of Featured Poets: Moonstone Poetry Series*.

HELD #2 and #1, under the title "Handlers," *Jasper*.

I am grateful to Swarthmore College for support in completing this manuscript; and to Herman Beavers, Abbe Blum, Cindi Boiter, Betsy Bolton, Syd Carpenter, Joy Charlton, Bob FitzSimons, Anthony Foy, Nzadi Keita, Kathryn Kirkpatrick, David Lloyd, Ed Madden, Marge Murphy, Lisa Sewell, Kristina Straub, and Elaine Terranova for comfort and advice.

With hope for a more embracing future for the region and the nation.

www.ingramcontent.com/pod-product-compliance
Lightning Source LLC
Chambersburg PA
CBHW071547080526
44588CB00011B/1822